Australian Cross-stitch Designs

Australian
Cross-stitch Designs

Vivienne Chinnery

Kangaroo Press

Acknowledgments

I wish to thank the following people, who with their help and encouragement have made it possible for me to produce this book.

To 'my' ladies from the Ocean Ridge Group of the Embroiderer's Guild of Western Australia; namely Helen McDonough who embroidered the colonial house for me, Meg Johnson, Irene Garrett, Hanna Reher, Jean Jenkinson, Jenni Kirkham, Eve San Filipo and Deborah Gerreyn.

To Dan Weir from The Needlewoman Shop in Perth for his patience and help in choosing the correct fabric, threads and colours.

To Bernard Prince from Novel Art Framers in Wangara, W.A. for a really professional job of framing all the pictures.

To Merle Davis for the loan of her treasured antique doll.

To Edward Garforth, who copied all the graphs with such infinite care.

Most of all to Lindsay Muskett, who took all the photographs in such a skilful and sensitive manner. Lindsay was able to understand perfectly what I wanted out of each photograph and to produce exactly what I had in mind. This book is as much his work as it is mine.

To my family, who have survived a year of living among graph paper, fabric, cottons, sketches and general chaos— my thanks and love.

Leigh, Pippa and Jackie; this book is from me to you.

Reprinted 1989, 1990 and 1991
First published in 1989 by Kangaroo Press Pty Ltd
3 Whitehall Road (P.O. Box 75) Kenthurst 2156
Typeset by G.T. Setters Pty Limited
Printed in Singapore by Kyodo Printing Pte Ltd

ISBN 0 86417 255 9

Contents

Preface

The idea for writing this book on simple, uncomplicated cross-stitch designs based on Australian themes grew from a group discussion by members of the Ocean Ridge Group of the Embroiderer's Guild of Western Australia.

While there seemed to be a variety of cross-stitch kits in the stores, there didn't appear to be books on Australian designs, suitable for working quickly and easily. A lot of women who enjoy working in cross-stitch have friends or relatives living in other countries and find it rather difficult to find small, original gifts to send 'home' for birthdays and Christmas. This book will provide many small designs that can be worked on any number of items and with very little time or effort involved.

The motifs, which are all original, can be combined, repeated or reversed, and used individually to provide a lot of scope for creating entirely new and unique ideas.

The designs can be adapted for use in tapestry work with wool, or even used as a motif on a knitted pullover or cardigan. Being simple, they can be done quite easily by young children without them getting bored.

I hope this book of Australian designs will give hours of pleasure to everyone who enjoys embroidery as much as I do... particularly cross-stitch.

Introduction

Cross-stitch is one of the most ancient of embroidery stitches. It appears in almost all traditional embroidery throughout the world, especially in European and Oriental national costumes, using brilliant coloured wools, silks and cottons.

It is a very simple, effective stitch and is formed by two diagonal bars, crossing at the centre.

Materials

Even-weave Fabric

Cross-stitch is nearly always worked over even-weave fabric, where the same number of threads are woven vertically and horizontally, and they are measured per inch of material. Aida cloth is readily available from most embroidery or craft shops, and comes in 11, 14, 18 or 22 threads per inch. Also, perhaps not so readily available, there are fine, even-weave linens, coarse-weave fabrics and Aida-band.

A design worked over 11 threads per inch will be twice the size of the same design worked over 22 threads per inch.

Your fabric should be at least 5 cm (2'') larger than the completed project on all sides to allow for mounting or finishing.

For instance, a 30 cm × 30 cm (12'' × 12'') picture requires a piece of fabric 40 cm × 40 cm (16'' × 16'') in size.

To keep the material from fraying, bind the edges with masking tape. Remove the tape when the embroidery is finished.

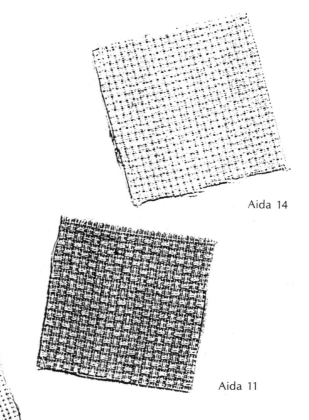

Aida 14

Aida 11

Aida 18

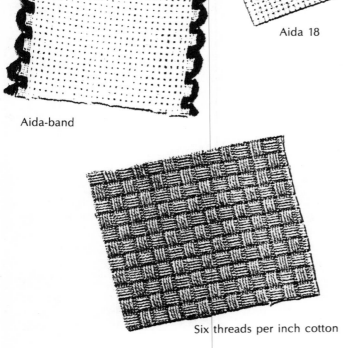

Aida-band

Six threads per inch cotton

Other Fabric

If the fabric to be embroidered is not a squared or even-weave fabric (such as towelling, fine cotton, even satin or velvet), a piece of tapestry or needlepoint canvas can be tacked on top and the design worked over this. After the design has been completed, the threads of the canvas can be pulled out, leaving only the cross-stitch motif. When doing this it is important to use woven, not bonded mono-canvas or needlepoint canvas, as bonded threads do not unravel when you try to remove them.

Thread

Stranded cotton comes in skeins of six strands. Separate the strands into three strands for 11 or 14 Aida cloth, two strands for 18 Aida cloth and one or two strands for 22 Aida cloth.

Needles

A blunt or ball pointed needle should be used, as this will slide easily into the corner holes of the squares in the cloth. Sharp needles can pierce the fabric and perhaps even cut into it, making an uneven cross-stitch.

Working on a Frame

While cross-stitch can be worked by simply holding the fabric in the hands, sewing is easier if the material is mounted on a frame to keep the fabric taut and the tension even.

Clean dry hands are important. It is very distressing after spending hours working on an embroidery, to find a grubby ring where you have held the embroidery hoop. If your hands begin to feel sticky or sweaty, wash them with soap, dry them thoroughly and dust them lightly with talcum powder.

Finally, always press finished work on the *wrong* side only, otherwise you will squash and distort the stitches.

Two types of frames are available—the ring frame and the slate frame.

Ring Frame

This consists of two rings—a smaller inner ring and a larger outer ring with an adjustable clamp. These rings or 'hoops' are generally made of wood, although more recent variations include plastic rings with a rigid inner hoop, and a flexible outer ring which stretches over the top of the other, eliminating the need for bulky clamps or screws.

To mount the fabric, place the centre ring flat on a table and lay the material over this so the design area is centred. Push the outer ring over this, making sure the material is taut with no 'pleats'. To stop the work slipping while it is being worked, bind the inner ring with bias-binding, winding it over the ring until it is completely covered.

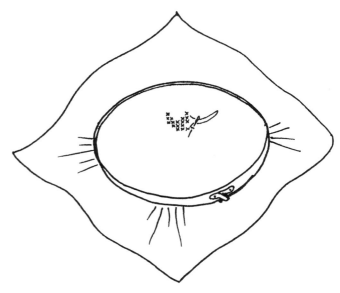

Ring frame

Slate Frame

The slate frame is made up of two dowels or rollers to which webbing has been attached with staples. Each roller is held between two bars and the corners are held together with long screws and bolts, or alternatively small clamps.

The material to be worked can only be as long as the webbing on the roller, but may be wider than the bars at the ends, as the surplus fabric can be wound around each roller, leaving an area to be embroidered exposed. As this area is completed, undo the screws at the ends, roll the work further onto the roller, enclosing a soft piece of flannelette material to protect your embroidery, and expose the next piece of fabric to be sewn.

To attach fabric to this type of frame, turn in a 1.25 cm (½'') hem to the wrong side at the top and bottom of the material. Match the centre point of the sides of fabric with the centre point of the webbing. Slip-stitch these sides to the webbing. Roll any excess material onto the rollers, then using a strong thread and a curved needle lace the top and bottom at 2.5 cm (1'') intervals: through the turnings, up and over the arms, and back through the turnings again. For best results, the material should be really firm and taut.

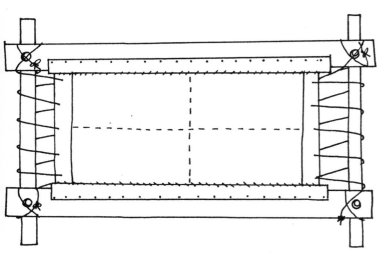

Slate frame

9

Methods of Working Cross-stitch

Method A

Starting at the bottom, left-hand corner for an individual square, take the needle from the back to the front of the work, and then at the upper right-hand corner of that square take the needle through to the back again. Work across the entire area of the design in this way, then return, going from the lower right-hand corner to the upper left-hand corner of each square to complete the crosses.

Always work horizontally with this method, not vertically, and do not change direction while working, or it will show up very clearly when the project is completed.

Work either from left to right or right to left, sewing the entire piece in the same way, in order to maintain an even tension.

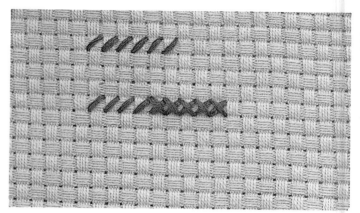

Method A

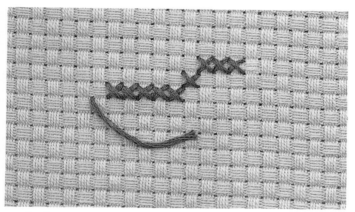

Method B

How to Start and Finish

Using cotton about 40 cm (16") long and a blunt needle, begin by leaving a 'tail' of thread at the back of the work and sewing the first few stitches over the top of it. NEVER start with a knot, or you will always have a lump on the front of your work to remember it by!

After you have sewn four or five stitches over the tail thread, cut off the excess thread.

To finish off a coloured thread, run the thread through the back of four or five stitches and cut off the remaining cotton.

Method B

When completed cross-stitches are to be worked individually, start at the lower left-hand corner of a square bringing the needle through to the front of the work, and then back again at the upper right, forward at the lower right and back at the upper left, bringing the needle forward again at the lower left-hand corner of the next square. This method is useful when working vertical and diagonal rows of stitches.

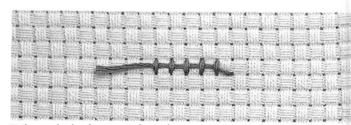

Tail caught by horizontal stitches

Tail caught by diagonal stitches

Half Squares

Sometimes a square is marked in such a way that each half square is to be worked in a separate colour. This is necessary to avoid a sharp corner effect on a curve, or it can be used when a pointed shape is to be accentuated.

Method:
Bring the needle from the back of the work to the front at the right-angled corner of the triangle to be filled in, taking it back again in the centre of the square. Bring the needle to the front again at the bottom corner and through to the back at the diagonally opposite corner. If the square is to be worked in two colours, repeat this method in the opposite triangle using the same holes.

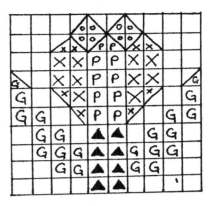

Working half squares

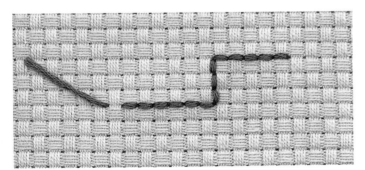

Backstitch

Straight stitch

Backstitch

This is a useful stitch for outlining. Work from left to right. Bringing the needle from the back to the front of the work one stitch-length in from the beginning of the line. Go to the back again at the start of the row. Next come to the front of the work one stitch-length ahead of the first stitch. See diagram.

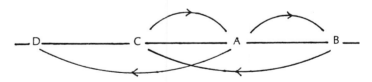

Sequence of working backstitch

Straight Stitch

Straight stitches are separate stitches formed by bringing the needle to the front of the work at the bottom of the stitch and to the back again at the top. These stitches are used for flower stamens, gum blossoms, grass etc., and do not always have to be of equal length or in the same direction.

Assisi Embroidery

Assisi in Italy, which is the birthplace of St Francis of Assisi, is also famous for the form of embroidery which bears its name.

With Assisi embroidery, the background of the design is worked in solid cross-stitch, leaving the design itself blank so that one can see fabric. This design is outlined in a darker coloured thread (usually black).

Assisi embroidery is done in two stages:

1. The outline.
2. The background.

1. The outline Begin by marking an outline in backstitch, one square at a time around the design area, around the border patterns and along any internal lines within the designs.

2. The background When the outlines are completed, fill in the background with cross-stitch working in horizontal lines. Take each line across the full width of the section being worked. NEVER 'hop' across the back of part of the design to arrive at a new section. End off each thread before starting a new section.

Backstitch outline only

Backstitch outline with only the background filled in—commonly called 'Assisi' work

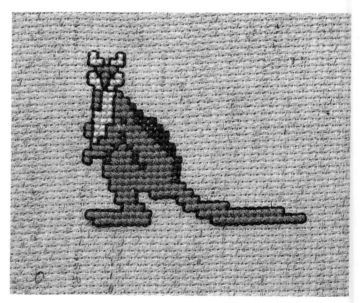

A cross-stitch design in several colours with a darker colour backstitch outline

Graphs

Each square on the graphs represents a single completed stitch, and each symbol represents a colour. Blank squares are left unworked. Check all the colours against the symbols on the list beside each graph design, before starting the work.

The centre of each design is marked with arrows on the top, bottom and both sides of the graph. Run a line of tacking stitches through these rows first, before starting to work. They can be removed later. Always begin at this central point.

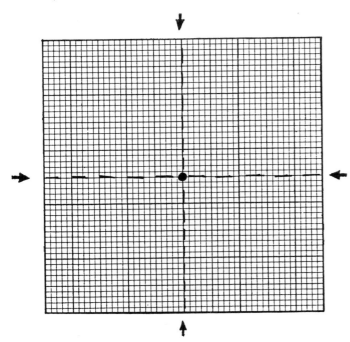

Finding the centre point

Stitch Count

'Stitch count' is the number of stitches both vertically and horizontally used to work a design. In this way, a picture or design can be made smaller or larger by using finer or coarser woven Aida Cloth.

Some patterns, however, must be done on the size I have recommended or the article (when finished) will not work out—e.g. the greetings cards would not fit the cardboard mounts if they were smaller or larger.

Some of the pictures are suitable for changing and these patterns feature a chart to show the different sizes on Aida cloth 11, 14 and 18, along with the stitch count.

Colours

For each project you will find a list of the colours that were used on the original items, as well as the manufacturer's number. Every effort has been made to accurately match the colours of each range, however it is really up to the individual to make the final choice.

If you would rather substitute bright colours for pastel ones, or use an entirely different shade of green from the one I have used, then feel free to do so. The colour code provided should be used only as a guide. It is the complete freedom of choice of colours, of size of Aida cloth, and of final presentation of work that makes embroidery such an individual and personal craft.

You will find that some designs are completely versatile. For instance when making the photo frame with red gum blossoms, if red doesn't suit your colour scheme, make them pink or yellow blossoms. The beautiful colours of nature are also extremely varied and versatile—the choice is all yours!

1. Three Wildflower Bookmarks

(See colour picture on page 17.)

Materials

Aida-band—50 cm (20'') makes three bookmarks
D.M.C. Stranded Cotton—cross-stitch worked with 3 strands.
Straight stitch and french knots worked in 2 strands.
All lettering is backstitched in 3 strands of black cotton.
Work the design at the bottom of the Aida-band, leaving
1.5 cm (⅝'') for the fringe and lettering at the top. When
finished, fringe and hem-stitch the ends.

Press with the embroidered side down.

Australian Wildflowers

Australia's position as an isolated island continent has
accounted for its unique and varied floral heritage. Several
extremes of climatic conditions—from dry, arid areas to
tropical rainforests; warm, open shrubland to cold snow-
covered mountains—have given us an astounding diversity
of wildflowers.

The flowers are so unlike those of any other continent,
that our early pioneers and explorers were generally
unimpressed. The European botanists of the time, however,
were enthusiastic about the discovery of such a vast array
of previously unknown plant forms.

In comparison to the flowers of the gentle English country
gardens, Australian flora is rather primitive and untamed.
Only in the last few decades have our own native plants
been accepted for their unique beauty, and cultivated for
use in Australian gardens.

Our wonderful heritage of unusual plants, after having
been thoughtlessly destroyed in huge quantities during times
of land-clearing, building progress and mining, is now being
protected for the future generations of Australians to enjoy.

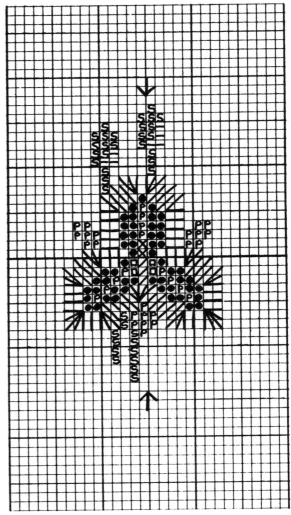

Fringe lily bookmark motif

Semco	D.M.C.		
924	367	S	dark green
923	368	~	light green
870	552	P	purple
868	554	●	mauve
926	472	▫	green
863	3689	∕	pink
	554	⚡	mauve straight stitch

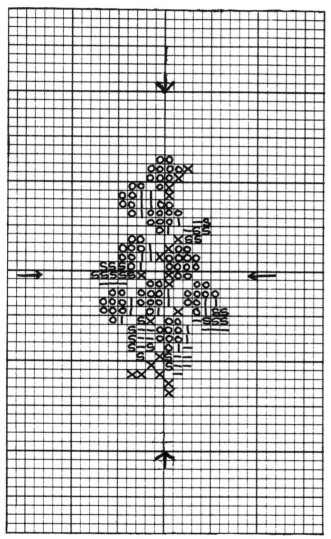

Golden wattle bookmark motif

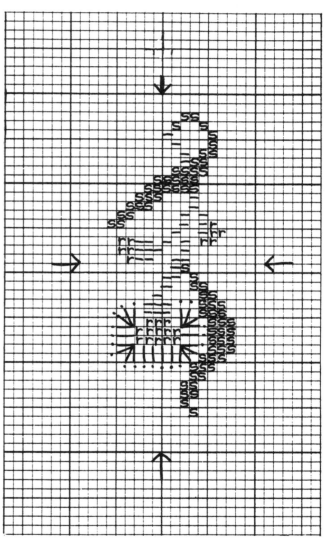

Red flowering gum bookmark motif

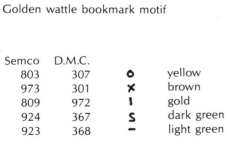

Semco	D.M.C.		
803	307	o	yellow
973	301	✗	brown
809	972	I	gold
924	367	S	dark green
923	368	—	light green

Semco	D.M.C.		
924	367	S	dark green
923	368	—	light green
839	350	r	coral
803	307	•	yellow
839	350	⬊	coral

2. Banksia Greetings Card

(See colour picture on page 24.)

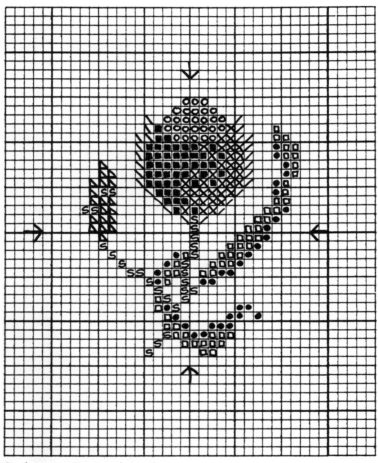

Banksia greetings card motif

Semco	D.M.C.		
806	745	o	pale yellow
809	742	▪	bright yellow
816	740	×	orange
816	740	⌄⌄	orange straight stitch
959	841	s	light brown
975	433	◿	dark brown
923	503	▫	light green
924	501	●	dark green

Materials

7 cm × 10 cm (2¾'' × 4'') Aida 14

Banksia

Named after the botanist, Sir Joseph Banks who accompanied Captain James Cook to Australia in 1770, banksias are unique to Australia. The size of the flowers can vary from 4 cm to 40 cm (1½'' to 16''), growing mostly on shrubs and small trees, although there are a few prostrate varieties. When the flowers die, a large woody cone develops holding the seeds for later release.

Three Wildflower Bookmarks (see page 14)

Gum Blossom Photo Frame (see page 31)

Australian Sampler (see page 64)

Aboriginal Painting Design (see page 44)

Monogram Bath Towel (see page 50)

Wattle and Grevillea Border (see page 49)

Gentleman's Residence (see page 54)

Squatter's Cottage (see page 56)

Parish Church (see page 58)

Wildflower Brooch (see page 60)

Pink and Grey Galah Picture (see page 36)

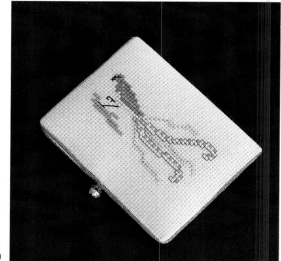

Lyrebird Needlecase
(see page 42)

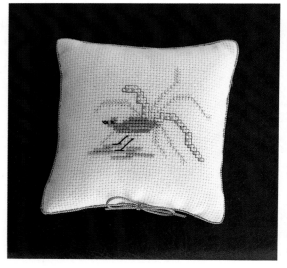

Lyrebird Pincushion (see page 41)

Lyrebird Scissors Case (see page 38)

Three Australian Butterflies Picture (see page 52)

Wild Orchid Cushion (see page 46)

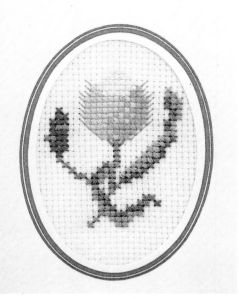

Banksia Greetings Card (see page 16)

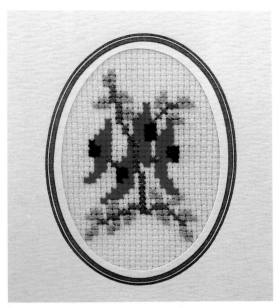

Sturt's Desert Pea Greetings Card (see page 26)

Red Capped Robin Greetings Card
(see page 27)

Honeyeater Greetings Card (see page 28)

Kangaroo Greetings Card (see page 29)

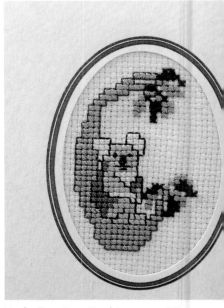

Koala Greetings Card (see page 30)

Instructions for Making Up
a Greetings Card

Cut thin cardboard into a rectangle measuring 33 cm × 15 cm (13½″ × 6″). Fold it equally into 3 sections each measuring 11 cm × 15 cm (4½″ × 6″). Cut an oval shape out of the centre section. Glue the cross-stitched motif behind the oval cut-out, then glue the left flap over the embroidery—be sure to glue only around the edges of the card. Care must be taken not to get any glue on the fabric.

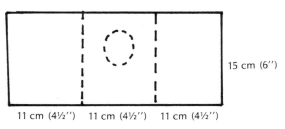

15 cm (6″)

11 cm (4½″) 11 cm (4½″) 11 cm (4½″)

Pattern for greetings card

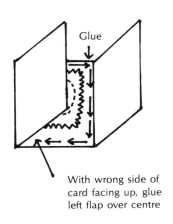

Glue

With wrong side of card facing up, glue left flap over centre

Assembling the greetings card

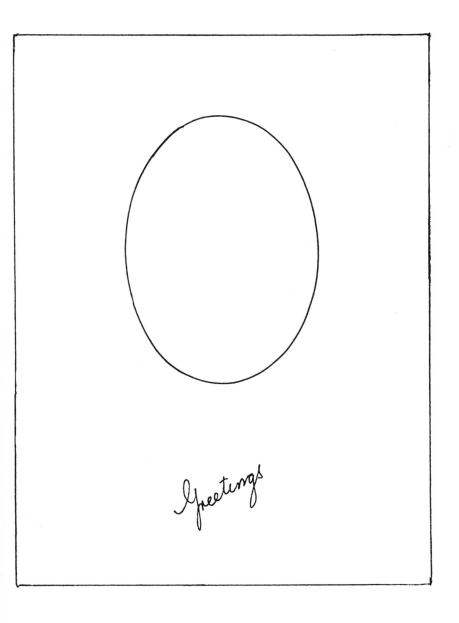

Greetings

Front of greetings card—actual size

3. Sturt's Desert Pea Greetings Card

(See colour picture on page 24.)

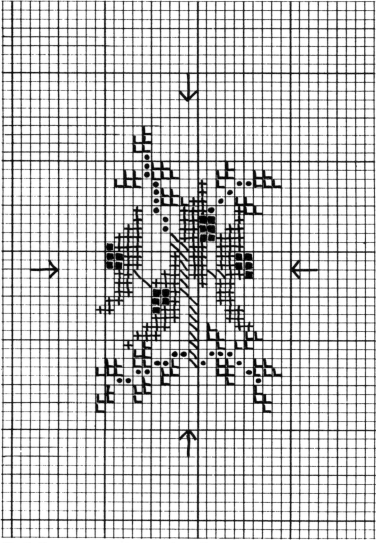

Sturt's Desert pea greetings card motif

Sturt's Desert Pea

Semco	D.M.C.		
923	368	L	light green
924	367	●	dark green
835	666	+	red
959	840	＼	brown
999	■		black

Sturt's Desert pea is a striking plant which, after rains in the dry areas, bursts into a mass of brilliant red and black flowers. The plant is a ground cover with soft grey-green leaves and stems. The seeds form in pods, but can lie dormant for long stretches of time between rains.

4. Red Capped Robin Greetings Card

(See colour picture on page 24.)

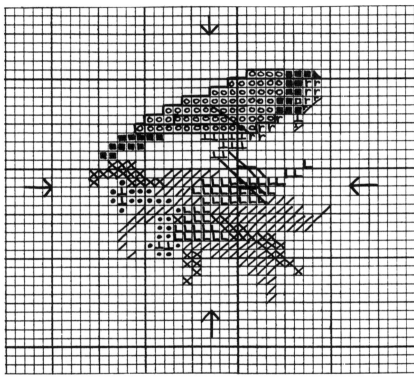

Red capped robin greetings card motif

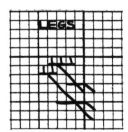

detail of legs

Semco	D.M.C.		
983	3022	o	brown
988	844	▣	charcoal
835	321	r	red
999	–	☐	black eye
961	436	⊥	light brown
946	937	✕	dark green
952	732	╱	medium green
943	3013	L	light green
964	433	•	rust brown
988	844	■	feathers and legs outlined in charcoal

Red Capped Robin

The red capped robin is the most widespread of Australia's red breasted robins, inhabiting the entire continent excepting the northwest, south coastal and rainforest areas. Robins hunt from low branches, catching insects and small lizards on the ground as well as flying insects and grubs from the trees.

5. Honeyeater Greetings Card

(See colour picture on page 24.)

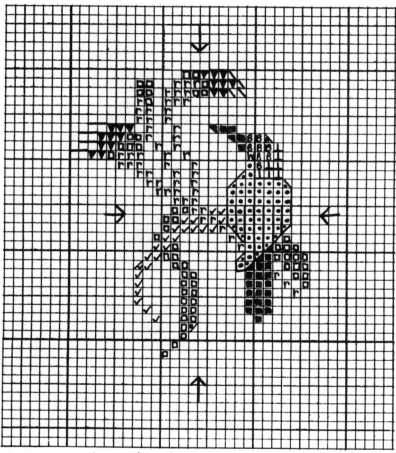

Honeyeater greetings card motif

Semco	D.M.C.		
942	470	□	light green
803	745	▼	pale yellow
835	321	┌	red
988	844	▪	outline feathers in charcoal
946	937	✓	dark green
999	–	╲╲╲ B	black
998	–	w	white
809	972	⊥	gold
989	318	●	grey
			red french knot for eye on centre 'B' stitch

Western Spinebill Honeyeater

Honeyeaters are small nectar and insect eating birds with a long, slender down-curved bill. The nectar and tiny insects are sucked up through a tubular tongue. Honeyeaters are abundant throughout Australia, helping to pollinate many of the unique flowering trees and wildflowers. The western spinebill is found in the southwest corner of the continent.

6. Kangaroo Greetings Card

(See colour picture on page 24.)

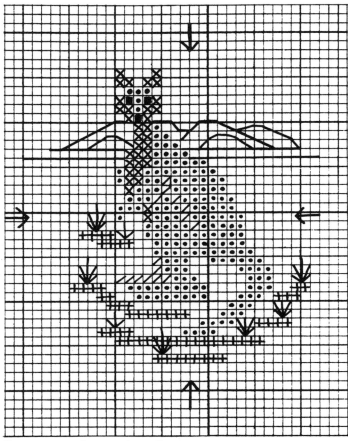

Kangaroo greetings card motif

Kangaroos

There are over forty species of kangaroos, wallabies and other relative mammals—all completely unique to Australia—the most common varieties being the grey and red kangaroos and the smaller wallaroo and wallaby. They live in small groups, feeding on grass and shrubs, and the leaves of small trees. Their very keen noses, ears and eyes warn them of danger from hunters or dingoes. Females carry their young in a pouch until quite developed. Even then, however, at the slightest hint of danger, the young kangaroo (or 'joey') will return immediately to its mother's pouch.

Rock wallabies and tiny rat kangaroos live in crevices in cliffs, dense thickets in scrubland and even in trees.

Semco	D.M.C.		
978	712	x	cream
959	3045	•	light brown
999		■	black
964	434	/	rust
950	581	+	dark green
949	472	⬇	light green
964	434	⌐	outline of kangaroo—one strand
949	472		outline of hills—two strands

7. Koala Greetings Card

(See colour picture on page 24.)

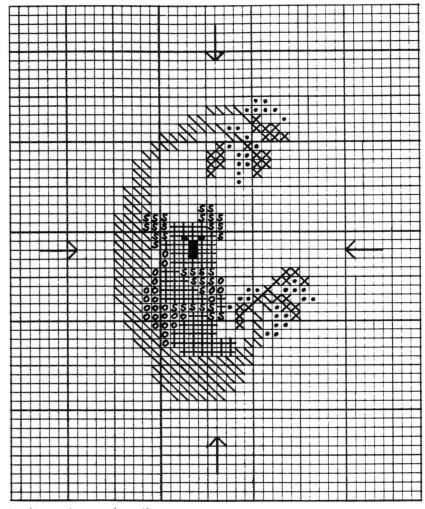

Koala greetings card motif

Koalas

Unique to this continent, koalas live in the eucalypt forests of eastern Australia, from the tropics to the cool-temperate zones. Koalas are not 'bears' as they are mistakenly called, but are related to the wombat. They are harmless, lovable looking animals, with soft greyish-brown fur and long claws, making it possible to climb the huge eucalypt trees that provide them with food and protection.

Semco	D.M.C.		
946	937	●	dark green
950	472	✗	light green
958	842	╲	fawn
985	762	+	silver grey
998		s	white
987	642	o	dark grey/brown
964	434	———	outline (tree) rust
988	535	∫	outline (koala) grey

8. Gum Blossom Photo Frame

(See colour picture on page 17.)

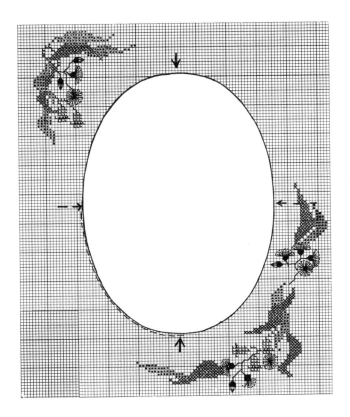

Eucalypts

Australia has over 450 species of eucalypts or, more commonly called, gum trees. Eucalypts range from twisted shrubs to huge towering forest giants, and the blossoms vary from large, showy red, yellow or coral coloured flowers, to clumps of tiny pale pink or white blossoms.

These trees can be found growing in all types of climatic conditions: in high, windswept snowy areas; dry, arid inland plains, and the cooler, more fertile coastal strips.

Eucalypts are important to the Australian environment, providing not only shelter and shade, but also food and in some cases water for the native animals and birds. They also provide the timber industry with a good quality hardwood.

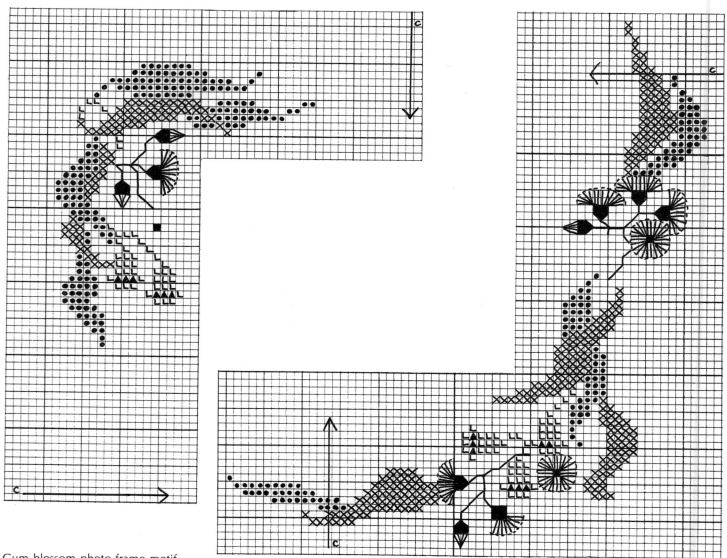

Gum blossom photo frame motif

Semco	D.M.C.		
943	644	●	light green
945	733	✕	dark green
980	841	L	light brown
947	935	■	bottle green
947	935		bottle green outline
834	351		coral pink straight stitch
800	307		yellow backstitch 1 thread
975	801		dark brown

Materials

2 pieces of thick white pasteboard 20.5 cm × 25.5 cm (8″ × 10″)
2 pieces of pasteboard for the stand
Tube of fabric glue
1 piece 10 mm (⅜″) thick quilt wadding 20.5 cm × 25.5 cm (8″ × 10″)
30 cm × 35 cm (12″ × 14″) Aida 14
30 cm (12″) calico cut to 24.5 cm × 29.5 cm (9¼″ × 11¼″)
1 m narrow gathered lace
12 cm (5″) length of 3 mm (⅛″) ribbon

Cut an oval centre from one rectangle of pasteboard. Carefully glue this rectangle to the wadding, and when dry, cut out the oval of wadding. Place the calico over the second rectangle of pasteboard so that there is a margin of 2 cm (¾″) all around. Trim the corners back to 1 cm (⅜″) and glue the edges over the pasteboard.

Repeat this process covering both pieces of stand with calico, leaving extra fabric on the top.

Being careful with the Aida cloth, remove the tape from around the edges. Leaving the tacking around the oval in place, cut around the oval to within 3 mm (⅛″) of the tacking line. Turn the edges over the wadding and pasteboard oval, and glue them into place.

Trim the corners back to 1 cm (⅜″) from the pasteboard, turn the edges over and glue them into place. Remove the tacking from around the oval when the glue is dry.

You now have one Aida frame shape, padded and embroidered, one calico back and two calico stands.

To assemble the frame:
Punch a small hole in the centre of one stand, thread the ribbon through and knot it on the wrong side. Glue both sides of the stand together, including the extra material on top. Making sure the bottom centre edges of both frame back and stand are even, mark a line on the frame back exactly the width of the top of the stand piece (excluding the material) and carefully slice along the line with a Stanley knife.

With the ribbon side in, slide the extra material through the cut, turn the flap down and glue it to the wrong side of the frame back. Punch another hole, this time in the back of the frame but level with the one in the stand, thread the ribbon through and knot it again on the wrong side.

Place the edges of the back and front of the frame together, and sew them up with tiny oversew stitches (one stitch per thread of Aida cloth), leaving the top open. Insert a photo and either leave the gap open or sew it up.

Glue narrow lace around the edges of the back of the frame.

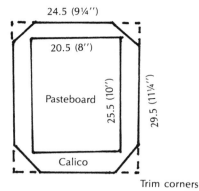

Covering frame with calico

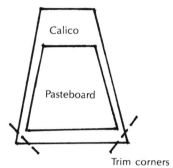

Covering stand with calico

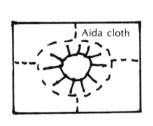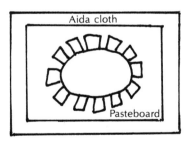

Covering frame with Aida

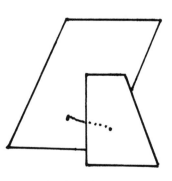

Back of frame

2 rectangles
2 stands

rectangle
cut 2

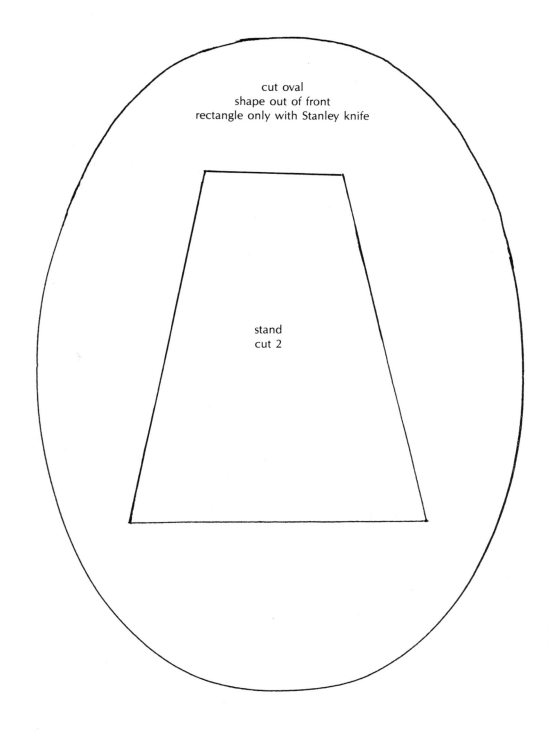

cut oval
shape out of front
rectangle only with Stanley knife

stand
cut 2

Actual size of cardboard for photo frame

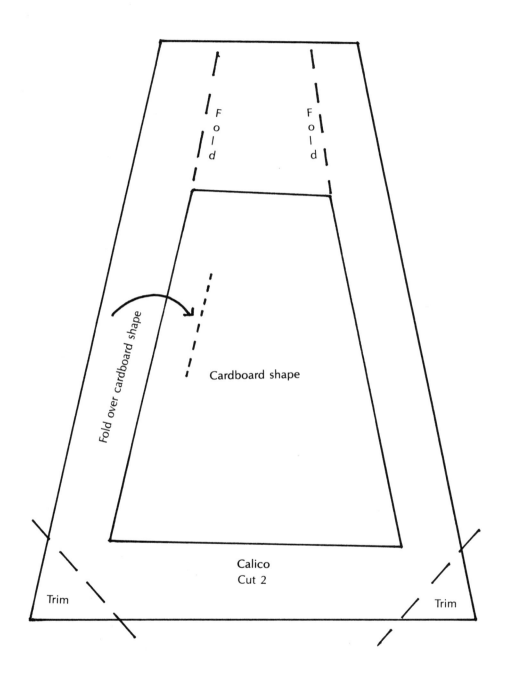

Fabric pattern for calico to cover stand

9. Pink and Grey Galah Picture

(See colour picture on page 22.)

Stitch count: 67 stitches × 58 stitches

	Motif size	*Fabric needed*
Aida 11	15 cm × 13 cm	42 cm × 30 cm
Aida 14	12 cm × 10 cm	26 cm × 23 cm
Aida 18	9.5 cm × 8.5 cm	22 cm × 20 cm

Galahs

Pink and grey galahs are members of the Cockatoo family. They thrive in large flocks, living in open, sparsely timbered inland areas, feeding on seeds, grasses and plant bulbs. Galahs have a very thick, strong beak suitable for digging up bulbs and cracking open hard seeds. Their talent for mimicking the human voice has made them popular household pets.

Semco	D.M.C.		
854	899	V	medium pink
855	335	P	rose pink
858	224	●	dusky pink
840	818	.	light pink
998	Blanc	/	white
986	415	\	dark grey
985	762	S	light grey
984	3022	ﻬ	grey/brown
979	842	◢	light brown
980	841	✕	dark brown
967	951	o	pale peach
965	3064	▲	rust
952	581	▢	dark green
944	472	∧	light green
976	801	✗	chocolate brown eye

Pink and grey galah picture motif

10. Lyrebird Scissors Case

(See colour picture on page 22.)

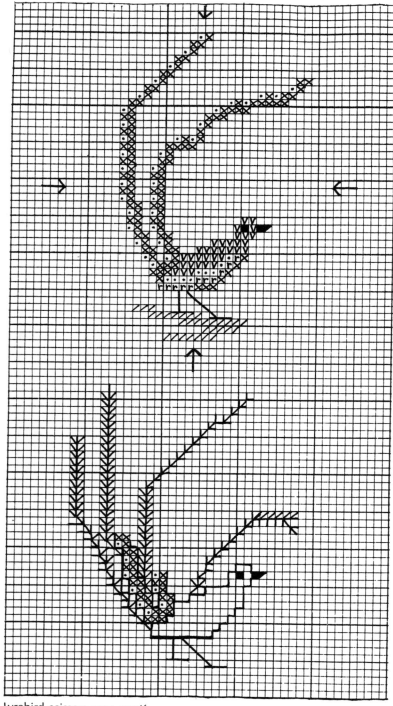

Lyrebird scissors case motif

Materials

2 squares Aida 14 each 12 cm X 14 cm (4¾'' X 5½'')
2 pieces lining fabric each 12 cm X 14 cm (4¾'' X 5½'')
Pasteboard for scissors case shape
Thin card for lining shape
48 cm (19'') plaited cord and 2 tassels
Using cardboard shapes mark 1 cm (½'') around all sides
with tacking stitches on the Aida cloth. To alleviate fraying
it is better when working on small projects to leave the
material intact until the embroidery is completed.

Place the thick card shapes in the centre of the Aida fabric
shapes and glue under the turnings. Using small stitches,
sew front to back RIGHT SIDE OUT, leaving the top open.

Repeat this process with the thin card and lining fabric,
sewing front to back RIGHT SIDE IN. Slip the lining into the
outer section, matching side seams, and sew around the top
section, joining the front of the lining to the front of the
needlecase, and joining the backs together in the same way.

Starting at the top corner, sew a plaited cord around the
edge to the opposite top corner, then around the top
opening edge. Finish off with tassles to hide the beginning
and ending points.

An alternative edging is a thin gold cord, available at most
stationery and card shops for the purpose of giftwrapping
presents.

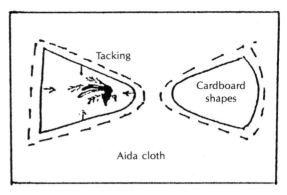

Tacking around the cardboard shapes on Aida cloth

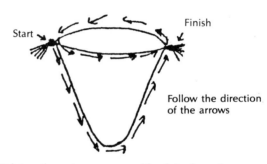

Edging the scissors case with plaited cord

Lyrebirds

Lyrebirds are only found in the cool temperate rainforest
areas of Queensland, New South Wales and Victoria. They
have a remarkable talent for imitating the calls of other birds
and wildlife. Female lyrebirds lay a single egg in a covered
nest among the ferns, while the male preens and spreads
his delicate silvery tail feathers that almost cover the rather
insignificant little brown bird underneath.

Semco	D.M.C.		
		∠	leg—dark brown
977	3031	■	dark brown
984	3032	V	light brown
953	ecru	X	cream
963	301	r	rust
961	436	•	honey brown
920	503	/	green
		↯	fine metallic thread
		↯	Lyre feathers outlined in rust

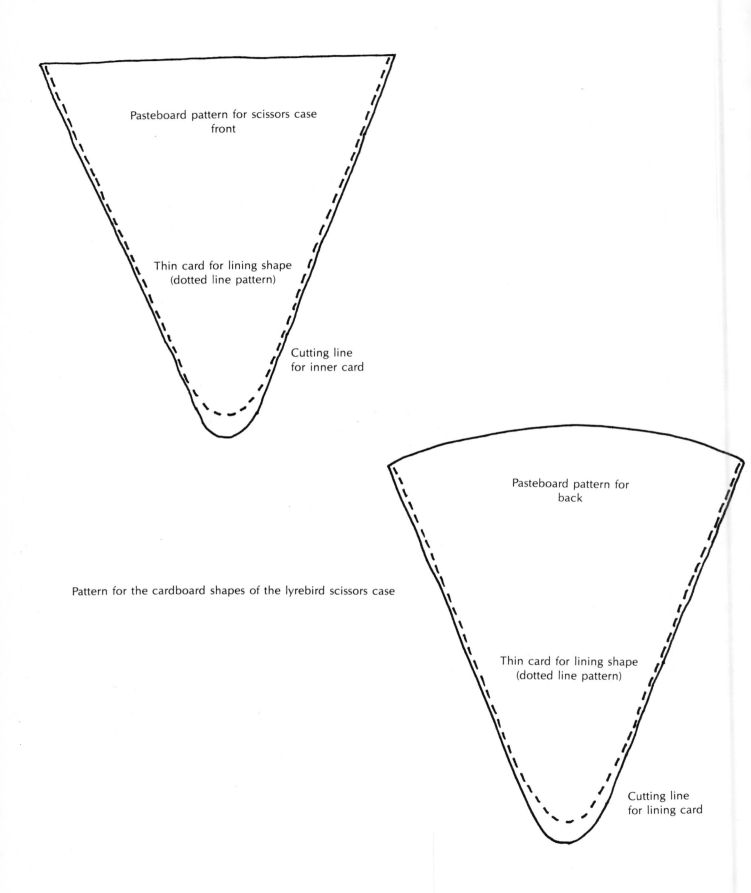

Pasteboard pattern for scissors case
front

Thin card for lining shape
(dotted line pattern)

Cutting line
for inner card

Pattern for the cardboard shapes of the lyrebird scissors case

Pasteboard pattern for
back

Thin card for lining shape
(dotted line pattern)

Cutting line
for lining card

40

11. Lyrebird Pincushion

(See colour picture on page 22.)

Cut a 14 cm (5½'') square of Aida 14 and tape the edges to prevent fraying.

Centre the design and work the cross-stitch motif, then using the graph, complete the metal thread tail feathers. Remove the tape.

Turn under 1 cm (⅜'') turning and slip-stitch the pincushion together on three sides. Fill it with wadding and sew the fourth side together. Make a plait using the remaining skein of green thread and slip-stitch around the edge of the pincushion, ending off with a small tassle.

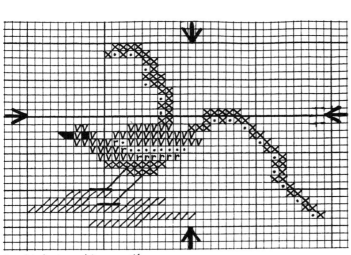
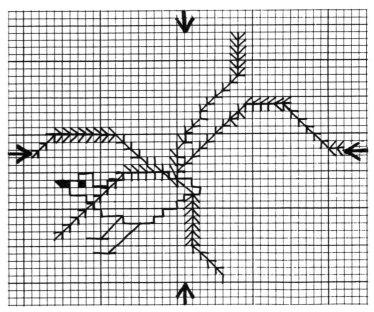

Lyrebird pincushion motif

Semco	D.M.C.		
		∠	leg—dark brown
977	3031	■	dark brown
984	3032	V	light brown
953	ecru	X	cream
963	301	r	rust
961	436	•	honey brown
920	503	╱	green
		↓↓	fine metallic thread
			Lyre feathers outlined in rust

12. Lyrebird Needlecase

(See colour picture on page 22.)

Materials

Aida 14—20 cm × 13 cm (8″ × 5″)
Pasteboard—18 cm × 11 cm (7″ × 4¼″)
Lining fabric—20 cm × 13 cm (8″ × 5″)
Flannelette—2 pieces 16 cm × 9 cm (6¼″ × 3½″)
10 mm (⅜″)thick wadding—9 cm × 11 cm (3½″ × 4¼″)
62 cm (24″) plaited cord
1 button
Mark the centre of all pieces of fabric and score a line across the centre of the cardboard.

Tape the edges of the Aida cloth and work the motif in one half of the material. Glue the wadding to one half of the pasteboard, lay the Aida cloth over this, with the motif over the wadding and turn over 1 cm (⅜″) turnings gluing them to the back of the card. Turn over 1 cm (⅜″) turnings on the lining fabric and slip-stitch around the edges, making sure all corners of the Aida and lining are even.

Fold the needlecase over in the centre and stitch both layers of flannelette down the centre seam.

Starting at the centre back, stitch some plaited cord around the needlecase, forming a loop at the centre front and sew a button at the joining point.

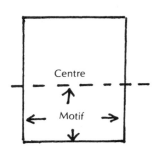

Marking the centre lines

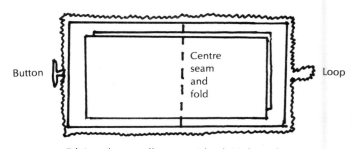

Edging the needlecase with plaited cord

Semco	D.M.C.		
977	3031	∠	leg—dark brown
984	3032	■	dark brown
953	ecru	V	light brown
963	301	X	cream
961	436	r	rust
920	503	•	honey brown
		⁄	green
		↡	fine metallic thread
			Lyre feathers outlined in rust

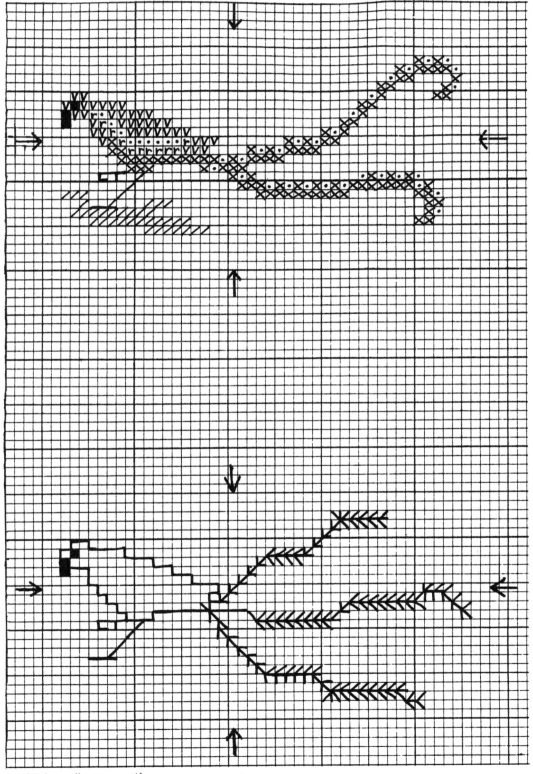

Lyrebird needlecase motif

13. Aboriginal Painting Design

(See colour picture on page 18.)

Stitch count: 46 stitches × 123 stitches

	Motif size	Fabric needed
Aida 11	10.2 cm × 27.3 cm	21 cm × 40 cm
Aida 14	8.4 cm × 22.4 cm	18 cm × 36 cm
Aida 18	6.6 cm × 17.6 cm	12 cm × 30 cm

Semco	D.M.C.		
976	838	✕	dark brown
971	919	•	rust brown
812	783	☐	gold brown
984	840	/	earth brown

Materials

18 cm × 36 cm (7″ × 14¼″) cream Aida 14
1 skein each of the four colours of stranded cotton
Backing board for the embroidered panel 11.5 cm × 28.5 cm (4½″ × 11¼″)
Heavy backing fabric (I used rust coloured upholstery fabric) measuring 25 cm × 43 cm (10″ × 17″)
Backing board, also measuring 25 cm × 43 cm (10″ × 17″)

Tack the centre lines vertically and horizontally in the Aida cloth and begin work from the centre point, using 3 strands of cotton throughout.

When the embroidery is completed, press it on the wrong side and stretch the fabric, using the lacing method, over the smaller backing board.

With fabric craft glue, adhere the backing fabric to the larger piece of backing board.

These simple preparations will make the framer's job a lot easier. This particular method of double framing is best left to a professional, as the embroidered panel has to be mounted on a block of wood, screwed to the centre of the backing board and framed in metal framing. The backing board is then framed and finished in the traditional way.

Aborigines

The Aborigines have inhabited this continent for over 40 000 years. They adapted to the harsh conditions of a predominently barren land with great skill, achieving a complete spiritual and practical harmony with the world around them.

They were basically nomadic people, living on the plants, animals, birds and fish that they hunted, while maintaining a great respect for the preservation of their environment.

Aboriginal art forms reflect this close association with nature. Rock paintings, bark paintings, and the decorations on their bodies, weapons and tools, signify the daily impact that the natural resources had on their lives.

The motifs in the panel have been adapted from Aboriginal paintings on bark, and can be used individually as well as collectively as shown. The colours were chosen to closely represent the natural tones of charcoal, ochre and vegetable dyes used originally.

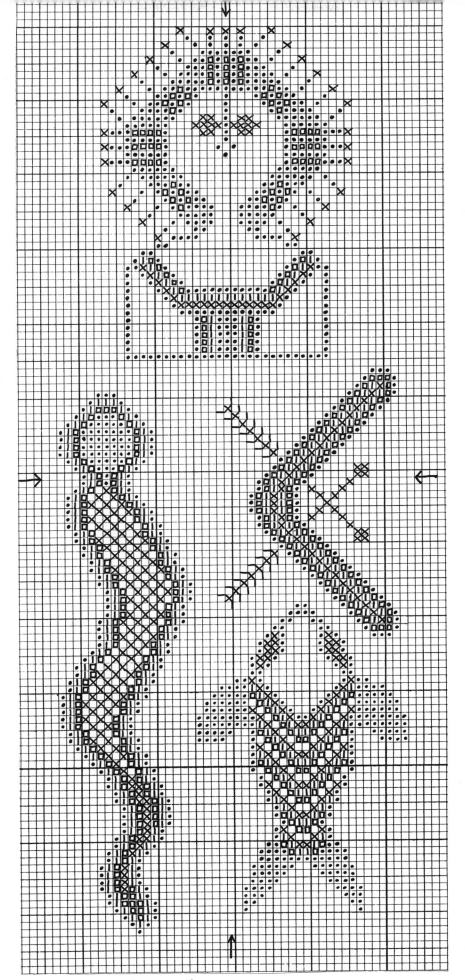

Aboriginal painting design motif

14. Wild Orchid Cushion

(See colour picture on page 23.)

Orchids

Orchids are regarded as one of the most interesting of plant families. There is such a great diversity among them, that some varieties do not appear to have anything in common with others.

Orchids such as donkey orchids, spider orchids, blue enamel orchids and the tiny pink fairy orchids are terrestrial. They die back each year, growing new leaves, underground tubers and new flowers each spring.

Other orchids such as orange blossom orchids, king orchids and ravine orchids grow in rock crevices, rotting trees and leaves etc., in the warmer areas of Queensland and northern New South Wales.

Some of the Australian orchids are small, ground hugging and completely insignificant to look at, but are just as perfectly adept in the unique methods of pollination as the larger, more flamboyant varieties.

Included in the design for the cushion (which would also look lovely worked in a finer cloth and framed) are spider orchids, donkey orchids, blue enamel and pink fairy orchids and large purple sun orchids.

Semco	D.M.C.		
869	208	I	violet
872	210	Z	mauve
947	935	Δ	bottle green
870	550	◢	bright purple
804	307	c	bright yellow
840	818	X	pale pink
842	776	◻	pink
843	899	N	rose
964	975	U	brown
971	920	r	rust
965	402	+	orange
998	Blanc	V	white
845	666	R	red
923	3053	•	grey/green
802	745	Y	pale yellow
877	327	P	purple
985	453	S	silver/grey
878	800	b	light blue
880	793	o	dark blue
980	841	F	fawn
951	470	9	dark green
928	368	▼	mid green
944	472	L	light green
807	744	•	yellow
808	725	■	mustard

Wild orchid cushion motif

Stitch count: 73 stitches × 129 stitches

	Motif size	Fabric needed
Aida 11	16.2 cm × 28.7 cm	30 cm × 37 cm
Aida 14	13.3 cm × 23.5 cm	24 cm × 28 cm
Aida 18	10.4 cm × 18.4 cm	16 cm × 26 cm

Materials

Aida 11 (ecru colour) 37 cm × 30 cm (14½'' × 12'')
1.5 metres (1.6 yards) ecru cotton lace 1.5 cm (⅝'') wide
Calico cut into the following sizes:

2 strips 43 cm × 5 cm (17'' × 2'') for the sides
2 strips 32 cm × 5 cm (12⅝'' × 2'') for the top and bottom
2 strips 43 cm × 8 cm (17'' × 3'') for the outer sides
1 square 43 cm (17'') for the back
3 strips 115 cm × 15 cm (45'' × 6'') for the frill
Polyester filling

Remove the tape from around the edge of the worked Aida cloth, and placing the fabric right side down on a padded surface, press with a damp cloth.

Tack the lace down the two sides of the work, leaving a 1.5 cm (⅝'') seam allowance. Lay calico strips 43 cm × 5 cm (17'' × 2'') over the top of the lace, level with the edge of the material and sew over the first tacking line.

Press the calico strips outwards, then repeat the process with the top and bottom, including the calico side strips in the seam.

Press all the strips outwards and sew the outer side strips down both sides with right sides together. Once again press them outwards. You will now have a square approximately 43 cm × 43 cm (17'' × 17''). Cut the backing piece to match. If you wish the cushion cover to be removable, cut the backing piece 46 cm × 43 cm (18'' × 17'') and insert a zipper across the centre before making up the cushion.

Join the three strips for the frill, fold in half lengthwise and press. Run a gathering thread around the length of the frill and pin it in place around the cushion front. Sew it in place, taking care not to catch the fabric at the corner.

Sew on the backing, leaving the bottom edge open. Turn the cushion right side out, fill it and slip-stitch the bottom edge closed. If using the zippered back piece, after sewing around all edges turn the cushion cover right side out, and insert a plain, pre-filled cushion.

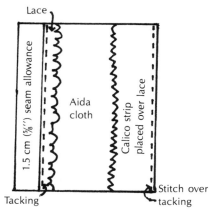

Attaching the lace and calico strips to the Aida cloth

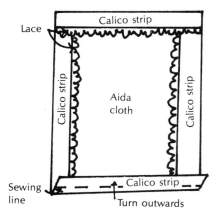

Pressing out the calico strips

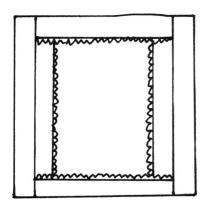

Attaching the outer side strips

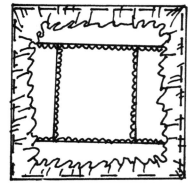

Attaching the frill

15. Wattle and Grevillea Border

(See colour picture on page 19.)

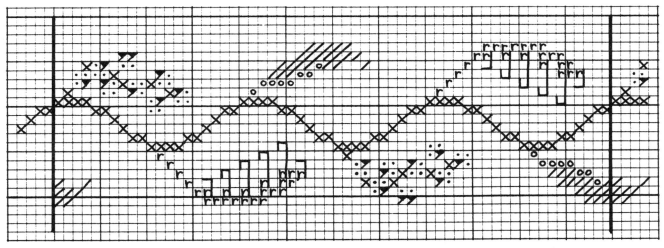

Wattle and grevillea border motif

Semco	D.M.C.		
960	437	✕	fawn
807	744	•	lemon
809	742	➤	gold
945	470	o	dark green
944	472	/	light green
839	352	r	pink
835	350	⌐	coral—outline

Embroidered Towels

Towels and facewashers become beautiful, personal gifts when they are embroidered with initials and motifs in any of the attractive colours now available in the stores.

When choosing towels for embroidery, the ones with the flat interwoven cotton strip at the end are the most suitable.

Cut a strip of evenweave fabric, the length and width of the motif to be embroidered and tack it into place on the flat band. Work the cross-stitch design, remove the tacking and then pull out the threads of the even-weave fabric, leaving only the embroidery.

Another method for embroidering towels, is to cross-stitch a border motif along a length of Aida-band and then slip-stitch this to the towel or facewasher after the embroidery is completed, making sure the ends are securely turned in and slip-stitched in place. Allow 4 cm (1½″) extra to the length of Aida-band for turning under at the ends.

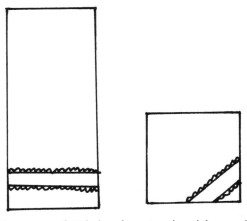

Placement of Aida-band on towel and facewasher

16. Monogram Bath Towel

(See colour picture on page 19.)

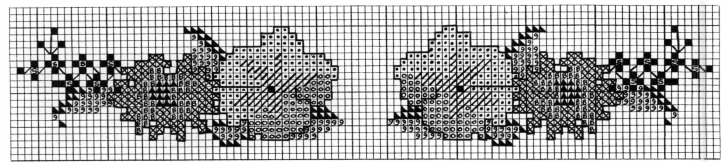

Monogram bath towel motif

Semco	D.M.C.		
807	744	■	pale yellow
975	938	`ı`	stems—one strand chocolate
949	734	◣	lime green
927	320	9	mid green
887	800	✕	light blue
889	798	B	dark blue
809	972	▲	gold
839	352	•	dark apricot
838	353	o	medium apricot
837	948	/	light apricot
816	741	s	deep gold
885	824		navy outline for blue flower
970	919		rust outline for apricot flower

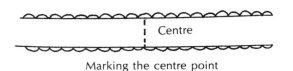

Marking the centre point

Using a piece of Aida-band 3 cm (1¼") wider than your towel, mark the centre point.

Calculate the number of spaces needed for your name or initials from the chart, adding spaces for full stops and leaving 5 spaces at each end between the flowers and the initials. For example the 'P.S.C.' on the page opposite has the number of squares needed for each letter and stop marked above it. This gives a total of 53 spaces. To find the centre point, divide by 2. If there is an odd number of spaces, the space left over will be in the centre thus:

26 + 1 + 26 = 53.

Count back from the central point to the start of the first letter and begin sewing. When the initials are completed, begin sewing the flowers from the middle outwards, reversing the second side.

When work is completed, press the Aida-band on the wrong side, slip-stitch it to the towel, allowing a 1.5 cm (⅝") turning at each end. Slip-stitch the ends in securely.

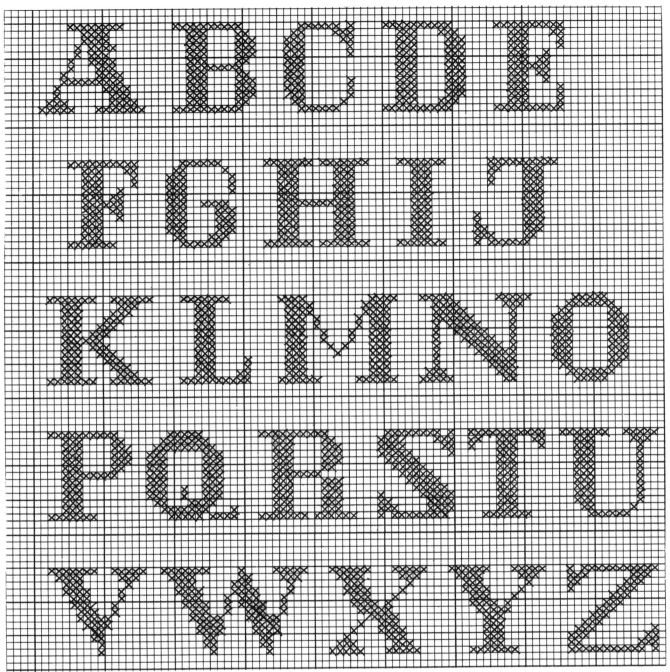

Chart of initials

Calculating the number of spaces needed

5 spaces	5
12 spaces for letter P	12
1 space	
2 spaces for full stop	} 4
1 space	
11 spaces for letter S	11
1 space	
2 spaces for full stop	} 4
1 space	
10 spaces for letter C	10
1 space	
2 spaces for full stop	} 3
5 spaces	5

17. Three Australian Butterflies Picture

(See colour picture on page 23.)

Stitch count: 68 stitches × 94 stitches

	Motif size	Fabric needed
Aida 11	15.1 cm × 21 cm	22 cm × 28 cm
Aida 14	12.4 cm × 17 cm	20 cm × 25 cm
Aid 18	9.7 cm × 13.4 cm	16 cm × 21 cm

Materials

16 cm × 21 cm (6¼'' × 8¼'') Aida 18 in cream or white
Oval frame measuring 11 cm × 16 cm (4¼'' × 6¼'')
Stranded cottons as suggested on the chart

Australian Butterflies

The first collection of butterflies from Australia was made by Sir Joseph Banks in 1770. His collection, which is still in the British Museum of Natural History, contains 36 species from the east coast.

While butterflies are found in all parts of Australia, the most exotic and colourful species are from the tropical areas of Queensland and more temperate New South Wales and Victoria.

I have singled out three completely different varieties of butterflies for the embroidery, taking particular care to include all markings.

Papilio ulysses is a bright metallic blue and black species, primarily from the tropical rainforest area of Queensland. It can be found from Cape York to Mackay, during most months of the year.

Papilio aegeus, commonly called the orchard swallowtail, is creamy yellow and black with red and blue spots on the lower wings. It inhabits the coastal areas of Queensland and vast areas of New South Wales and northern Victoria, and can be found during the summer months.

Vanessa kershawi, or painted lady, is a smaller variety in bright orange, black and gold colours. It can be seen throughout much of Australia, including Western Australia and Tasmania.

Great migratory flights take place in a general southerly direction across the country every spring.

Semco	D.M.C.		
999	310	■	black
875	550	/	purple
957	739	o	cream
896	517	•	turquoise
905	518	L	aqua
881	796	◢	royal blue
975	839	▲	chocolate brown
961	437	6	light brown
950	470	x	green
949	472	϶	lime
946	937	▼	bottle green
998	Blanc	w	white
821	970	∧	orange
816	972	G	gold
894	813	s	blue
845	349	r	red
801	746	Y	pale yellow
983	842	м	medium brown

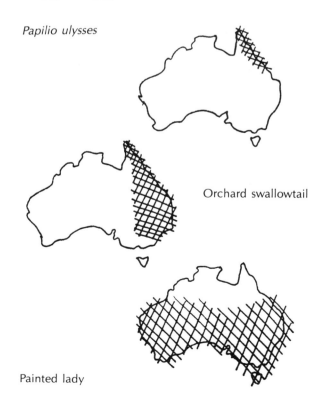

Papilio ulysses

Orchard swallowtail

Painted lady

Three Australian butterflies motif

18. Gentleman's Residence

(See colour picture on page 20.)

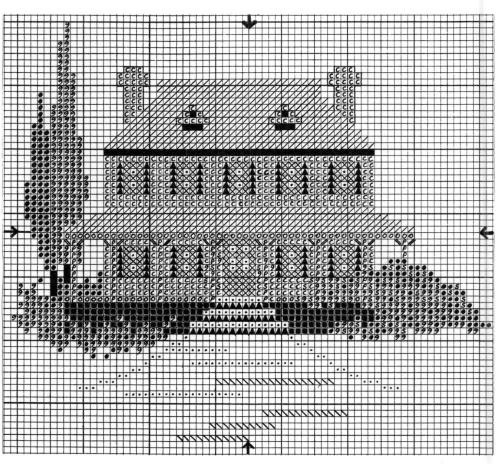

Gentleman's residence motif

Semco	D.M.C.		
950	469	●	dark green
943	472	9	light green
981	ecru	c	cream
986	415	/	grey
983	841	◾	brown
825	353	▲	apricot
987	646	✕	dark grey
824	754	•	light apricot
905	932	o	blue
990	3041	P	purple (grey)
863	3689	S	pink
823	948	\	very pale apricot
990	3041	＼ ∥	purple straight stitch

Stitch count: 73 stitches ✕ 66 stitches

	Motif size	Fabric needed
Aida 11	16 cm ✕ 14.7 cm	44 cm ✕ 32 cm
Aida 14	13.3 cm ✕ 12 cm	34 cm ✕ 28 cm
Aida 18	10.4 cm ✕ 9.4 cm	25 cm ✕ 21 cm

Gentleman's Residence

In the early nineteenth century, with the introduction of dairy cattle and sheep farming, the 'landed gentry', such as John Macarthur (the father of the Australian Wool Industry) were granted large land holdings. With the use of convict labour, they prospered and accumulated great wealth and prestige in the colony.

Chosen for the embroidered picture is a typical two storey home, with huge fireplaces, landscaped gardens and shuttered windows, with large shady verandahs to protect the expensive decorations and furniture from the harsh Australian summer. This type of residence would have been surrounded by various outbuildings, such as stables, convict housing and servants' quarters, carriage house, blacksmith shop and storage sheds.

Instructions for Making Up a Picture of Colonial Buildings

Materials

34 cm × 28 cm (13½″ × 11″) of cream Aida 14
34 cm × 28 cm (13½″ × 11″) calico backing fabric
20 cm × 25 cm (8″ × 10″) backing cardboard
Cardboard frame with oval cut-out—sometimes these are available pre-cut from photographic suppliers, otherwise carefully cut your own.

Before sewing the picture, make sure the design is centred properly. When you have completed the embroidery, press it on the wrong side, using a soft towel padding to prevent the stitches getting flattened.

Lay the calico and embroidered Aida cloth over the cardboard backing and lay the framed oval cut-out over the two. When the picture is placed correctly in the centre of the oval, lace the material and calico (together) around the cardboard, tightly.

Place the oval cut-out in place and frame with a narrow frame.

Actual
size of oval cut-out

Pattern for cardboard frame for colonial buildings

19. Squatter's Cottage

(See colour picture on page 20.)

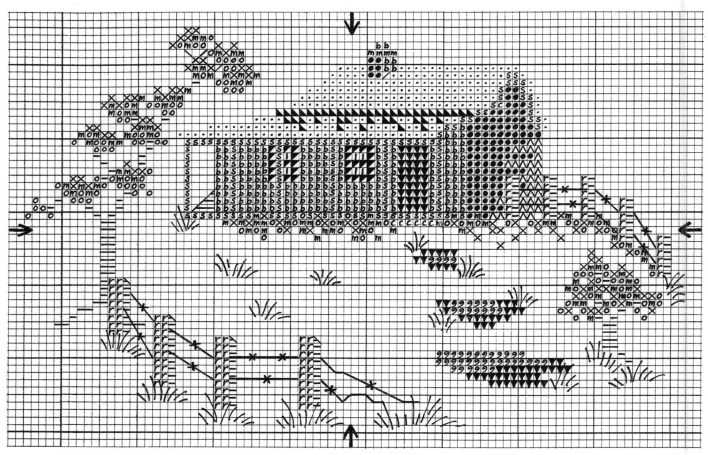

Squatter's Cottage motif

Stitch count: 87 stitches × 55 stitches

	Motif size	Fabric needed
Aida 11	19.3 cm × 12.2 cm	44 cm × 32 cm
Aida 14	15.8 cm × 10 cm	34 cm × 28 cm
Aida 18	12.4 cm × 7.8 cm	25 cm × 21 cm

Semco	D.M.C.		
999	310	✗	black outline—2 strands
809	742	9	gold
976	898	c	chocolate brown
894	932	I	light blue
973	433	—	dark brown
897	930	▼	dark blue
823	951	Λ	pale apricot
943	369	×	light green
945	368	M	mid green
951	469	o	dark green
986	318	·	grey
953	739	●	cream
958	437	b	fawn
825	353	▼	deep apricot
985	762	▲	silver grey
984	642	s	brown
971	918	r	rust

Squatter's Cottage

Poor settlers—labourers, ex-convicts and small farmers—moved with their families away from the growing city of Sydney and into the bushland, where they cleared land for themselves, grazed sheep and cattle, grew crops and 'squatted'. The squatters were a hardy breed; the epitome of 'pioneering spirit'.

They would have lived in tents and hastily constructed shelters at first, but as the need for a more permanent form of housing arose, the settlers were forced to use materials on hand to build their dwellings.

A framework of timber was used, filled in with slabs of woven wattle twigs and covered with a mud mortar. The roofs were made of thatched rushes and reeds, and a brick chimney standing away from the general dwelling completed the basic, but practical, squatter's cottage.

20. Parish Church

(See colour picture on page 20.)

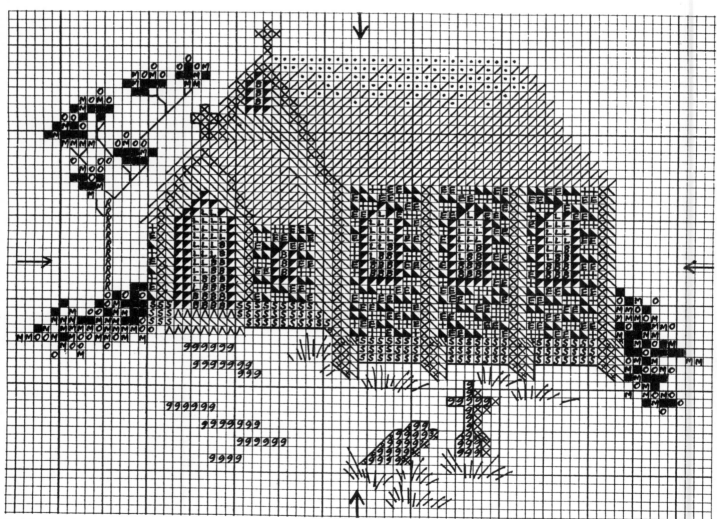

Parish Church motif

Stitch count: 78 stitches ✕ 57 stitches

	Motif size	*Fabric needed*
Aida 11	17.3 cm ✕ 12.7 cm	44 cm ✕ 32 cm
Aida 14	14.2 cm ✕ 10.4 cm	34 cm ✕ 28 cm
Aida 18	11 cm ✕ 8 cm	25 cm ✕ 21 cm

Parish Church

The first church service was conducted on Australian soil under some trees on Sunday 3 February 1788, by Reverend Richard Johnson, in the presence of soldiers and convicts.

In 1817 the first of several fine colonial churches was begun. St Matthew's church in Windsor, was followed in 1818 by St Luke's in Liverpool and it wasn't long before most settlements boasted their own parish church.

These were built using convict labour, which did not detract from the excellent workmanship. Beautiful interior finishings, colourful glass windows and magnificent altarpieces were a labour of love for some men who, nearing the end of their time, took absolute pride in their work. Many of these old churches are still standing today, and examples of this fine work with such close attention to detail, rivals any of the modern churches built in recent times.

½ cream ½ honey	
½ stone ½ cream	
½ honey ½ fawn	
½ honey	

Semco	D.M.C.		
987	414	╱	grey
985	762	·	silver
943	369	o	light green
945	368	M	medium green
951	469	■	dark green
812	437	x	honey brown
984	611	▼	brown
897	930	B	blue
894	932	L	light blue
953	739	╲	cream
981	644	s	stone
975	801	R	rust brown
978	842	9	fawn
966	951	◣	light brick
967	945	+	medium brick
968	353	E	dark brick
968	353	▵	dark brick
945	368	⩟	straight stitch medium green

21. Wildflower Brooch

(See colour picture on page 22.)

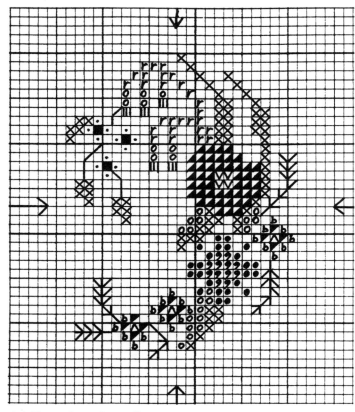

Wildflower brooch motif

Included in the design for this brooch are several wildflowers from all over Australia. The kangaroo paw, and native wistaria, from Western Australia, golden guinea flower from Victoria and Tasmania, the desert rose from the interior of the Northern Territory, Queensland and New South Wales, and blue leschenaultia from the southwest of Western Australia.

Enlarged this would look lovely in a picture frame. Here are the details to work out the size for enlargement:

Stitch count: 25 × 33 stitches

	Motif size	Fabric needed
Aida 11	5.6 cm × 7.3 cm	11 cm × 15 cm
Aida 14	4.5 cm × 6 cm	9 cm × 12 cm
Aida 18	3.6 cm × 4.7 cm	6 cm × 8 cm

Materials

6 cm × 9 cm (2⅜″ × 3½″) white Lugano fabric which has 26 threads per inch
Brooch frame with a 4 cm × 3 cm (1½″ × 1¼″) oval
Cardboard shape cut to fit the brooch frame
Small piece of polyester filling

Work the embroidery in the colours suggested on the chart. The design is worked in two strands, with the brown stems and leaves done in one strand. Cut the material 1 cm (⅜″) larger than the cardboard shape. Place the polyfil wadding on the oval shape, cover it with the fabric and lace tightly across the back, pulling the embroidery taut. Glue this shape into the brooch frame.

Semco	D.M.C.		
951	470	X	dark green
949	472	o	light green
845	349	r	red
872	211	·	pale mauve
874	209	■	dark mauve
850	776	◢	pink
860	3685	v	maroon
894	519	♭	blue
896	517	▼	dark blue
999	310	△	black
803	307	•	yellow
809	972	9	gold
974	801	↗	brown
999	310	)))	black straight stitches

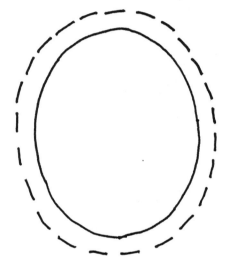

Cut the fabric 1 cm (⅜) larger all round than the cardboard shape. Place wadding between the two.

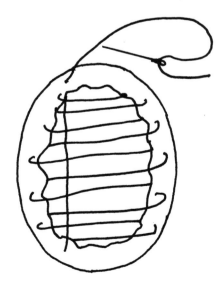

Turn the fabric over the edge of the cardboard shape and lace tightly to make the embroidery taut

Colonial Fashion

Never in the history of Australian female fashion was there such a contrast between rich and poor as in the early days of this colony. While the wives of the officers and soldiers dressed with all the frills and finery of their counterparts in England, the convict women wore dresses of coarse, natural coloured linen and woollen fabrics, with little, if any, adornments. However with the aid of printed fabric kerchiefs, pieces of lace and ribbon, even cheap articles of jewellery such as brooches, pendants and the like (which were treasured and coveted), some managed to take a pride in their appearance.

In direct contrast, the upper classes wore dresses of silk, satin, muslin and fine cotton, often brought by ships from London and Paris. These were trimmed with lace falling from the sleeves, lace-edged kerchiefs, underskirts with lace frills and lacy little mob caps. Mob caps were worn, both inside and out, making a soft, flattering frame for the face. Bodices were form fitting and worn over full skirts, covering several copious petticoats. Sleeves were full, or else worn tight with full frills around the lower arm. Dainty muslin kerchiefs covered the shoulders and fastened at the front with a jewelled pin or brooch. While these brooches or pins were often of precious stones set in gold and silver frames, there have been examples of very finely embroidered brooch centres, in beautiful silk threads on the finest of linen fabric. These would certainly have held an important position in a lady's wardrobe!

To protect the fair English complexion from the harsh Australian sun, bonnets were worn at all times out of doors. These were trimmed with ribbons, flowers—both artificial and fresh, jewelled combs and enormous ostrich feathers. In all, the convict women were probably quite a bit more comfortable in their largely uncluttered styles, than the mistresses they served!

22. Small Christmas Decorations

(See colour picture on page 21.)

These fun little Australian characters are extremely quick and easy to work. They look absolutely beautiful on the Christmas tree if finished off with gathered lace or a frill of Christmas print fabric, and a chirpy red bow.

For each decoration, you will need:

1 × 6 cm (2½'') diameter flexible plastic embroidery hoop
10 cm × 10 cm (4'' × 4'') white Aida 14
50 cm (20'') lace approximately 2 cm (¾'') wide, or 50 cm × 5 cm (20'' × 2'') Christmas print fabric, folded lengthwise
50 cm (20'') red ribbon, cut into three pieces:
   1 × 24 cm (9½'') for loop
   1 × 12 cm (5'') for small bow
   1 × 14 cm (5½'') for large bow
6 cm (2½'') circle of cardboard covered by a 9 cm (3½'') circle of print fabric

Stretch the fabric into the flexible hoop and work the outline first, using two strands of black stranded cotton. Fill in the design, using the colours in the graph, and three strands of cotton.
   Trim the fabric close to the back of the hoop. Gather the lace or frill and glue it to the back of the circle, sewing the ends together to neaten it. Cover the cardboard circle with glue, place it in the centre of the fabric circle. Clip the edges of the material and press them down around the circle. Glue the cardboard circle to the back of the frill. Sew a loop and a small bow to the top of the decoration, and glue a larger bow to the bottom.

Using the decoration instructions for the previous designs, substitute emerald green ribbon for the red ribbon used.

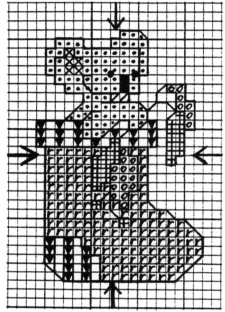

Koala in a stocking motif

Semco	D.M.C.		
986	648	•	grey
967	948	×	apricot
968	402	╱	peach
944	472	o	light green
945	469	+	dark green
809	973	▼	gold
845	666	r	red
			outline—two strands black

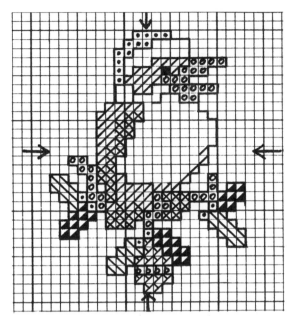

Kookaburra in a Christmas tree motif

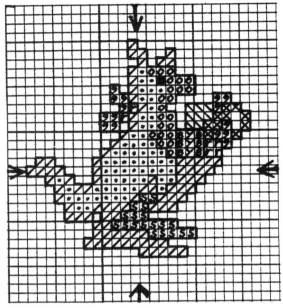

Kangaroo with a pouch full of presents motif

Semco	D.M.C.		
845	666	•	red
960	841	╱	light brown
984	3022	o	fawn
975	839	✗	dark brown
926	369	╲	light green
930	700	◢	dark green
–	–		blank—unworked
–	–		outline in two strands black
807	744	Y	yellow
895	996	♭	blue

Semco	D.M.C.		
974	433	╱	dark brown
984	3032	•	mid brown
961	407	o	honey
868	210	╲	mauve
896	996	B	blue
803	744	Y	yellow
914	700	9	green
845	666	r	red
843	956	✗	pink
999	–	■	black
999	–	▬	black
976	838	S	chocolate

23. Australian Sampler

(See colour picture on page 18.)

A sampler is traditionally a record of families, lifestyles, buildings, places, animals, birds, flowers etc. They have been worked to commemorate weddings, births, coronations and even wars.

This particular sampler has been designed to commemorate Australia's Bicentennial, but would look just as colourful and attractive with the family name and the year of sewing inserted at the top instead.

Included are gumnuts, gum blossoms, a kookaburra, a ring-tailed possum, a koala, a black swan, a parrot and a platypus, with a map of Australia and a traditional Australian homestead.

Across the bottom of the sampler is a native grass tree (commonly called a blackboy), the floral emblems of each state (see below) and the national floral emblem, wattle.

New South Wales—waratah
Queensland—Cooktown orchid
Victoria—pink heath
South Australia—Sturt's desert pea
Western Australia—kangaroo paw
Tasmania—blue gum
Northern Territory—desert rose

Samplers can be very colourful pieces of work, as well as being a practical way of using up all those half-used skeins of cotton that seem to collect in sewing boxes.

For this reason, I have not specified any colour code numbers, merely listed the colours as 'dark brown', 'mid green', 'red' etc.

Materials

Cream Aida 14 measuring 55 cm × 45 cm (22″ × 18″)
Backing board 31 cm × 41 cm (12″ × 16″)
Various colours of stranded cotton (use three strands throughout with outlines worked in one strand only)

To centre the family name and date, chart the letters from the alphabet graphs on page 71, count the number of squares, divide by two and work an even number of squares either side of the central mark. If the word has an odd number of letters sew the central square over the centre mark.

Total 41 squares

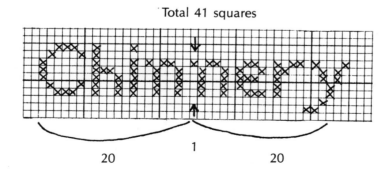

20   1   20

Total 18 squares

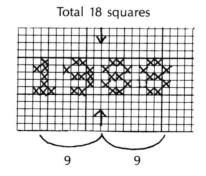

9   9

Example of centering

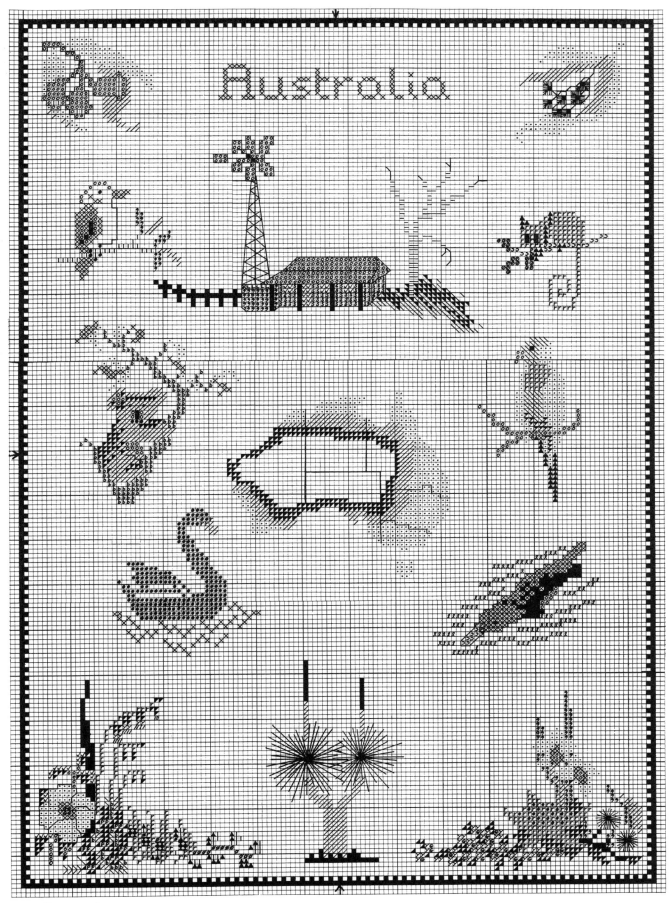

Australian sampler

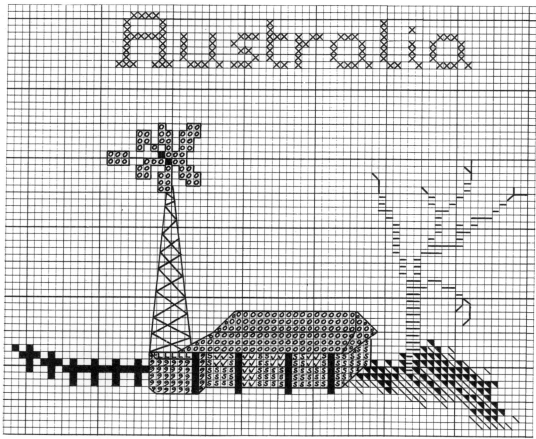

Australian homestead motif

x red
o fawn
■ dark brown (outline—1 strand, tank stand—2 strands)
L light blue
9 silver grey
✓ dark blue
— mid brown
\ olive green
▼ light olive green
s apricot
   tank outlined in 1 strand dark blue

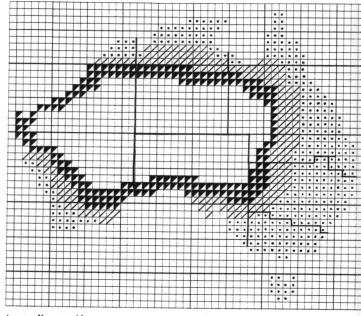

• olive green
▼ burnt orange
/ gold
   outline—1 strand of chocolate brown

Australia motif

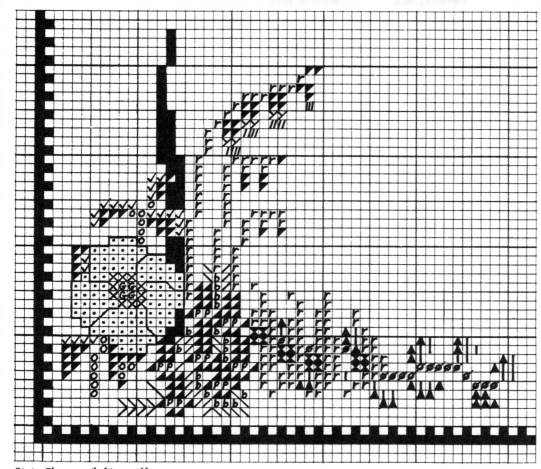

State Flowers (left) motif

■ dark green
⌐ mid green
√ light green
· pale pink
ᵷ golden yellow
✗ maroon
ᴑ light brown
ᕼ brown
ᵣ red
∅ grey/brown
ᴘ medium pink
◢ rose pink
✗ black
▲ dark bluish/green
ᴵ light bluish/green
✗ dark green

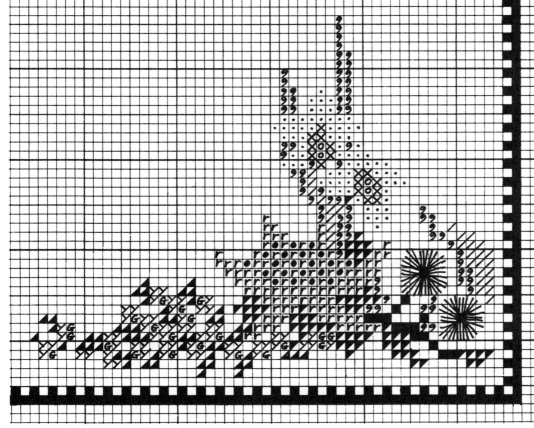

State Flowers (right) motif

ᵧ light olive green
⁄ dark green
· mauve
✗ purple
ᴑ light orange
ᵣ red
• coral pink
ᵧ yellow
ɢ golden yellow
■ chocolate brown
(outline around
wattle 1 strand)
※ pale blue straight
stitches—2 strands
⌐ mid olive green
◢ light grey/green

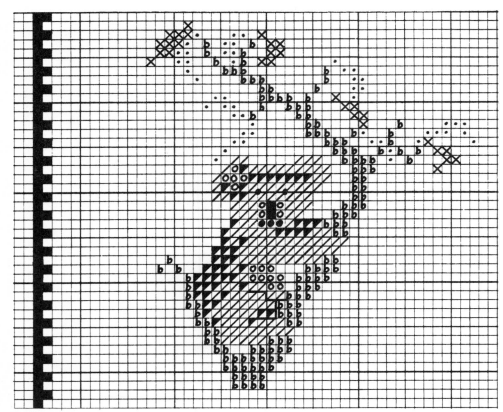

Koala motif

/ silver grey
▼ grey/brown
o white
● black eyes
● apricot
b brown
• light green
✗ dark green

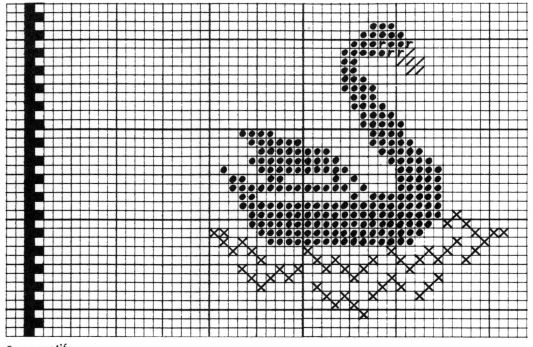

Swan motif

● black
r red
/ maroon
✗ blue
Leave open squares blank

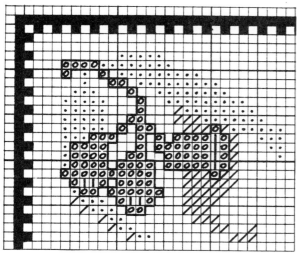

Gumnut motif

edging—chocolate brown
- · light blue/green
- / dark blue/green
- o fawn
- ı brown
- outline—1 strand chocolate brown

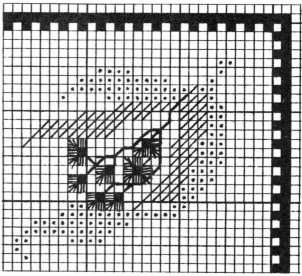

Gum blossoms motif

- · light blue/green
- / dark blue/green
- ⟋⟋ stems—brown
- ▪ dark brown
- 🖌 coral pink—1 strand

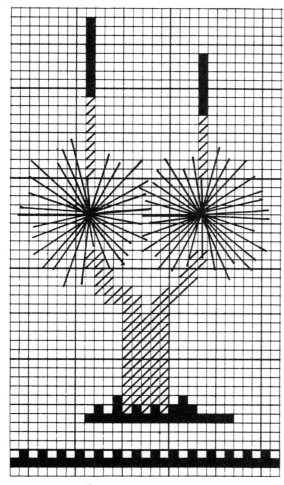

Blackboy motif

- / olive green
- ▪ light brown
- Flowers—long straight stitches in 1 strand each of light olive green, medium green, and bottle green

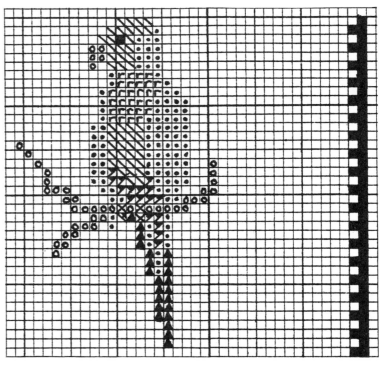

Parrot motif

- ＼ royal blue
- · 2 strands lime green with 1 strand yellow
- ▪ black
- o brown
- ⌐ 2 strands orange with 1 strand red
- ⅂ yellow
- × chocolate brown
- ▲ 2 strands olive green with 1 strand lime

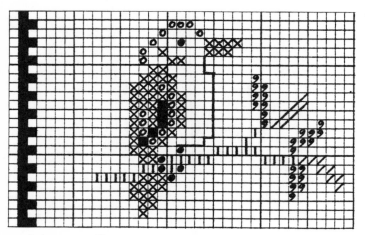

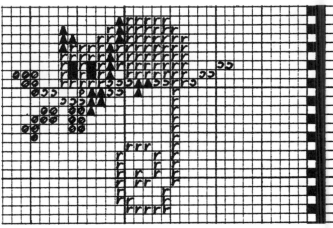

Kookaburra motif

O light brown or fawn
✕ medium brown
▪ electric blue
ı grey
9 olive green
╱ light olive green
● black
╘ outline—2 strands medium brown

Possum motif

P pink
r rust
▲ fawn
つ grey/brown
∅ pale green
▪ black
  outline in 1 strand very dark brown

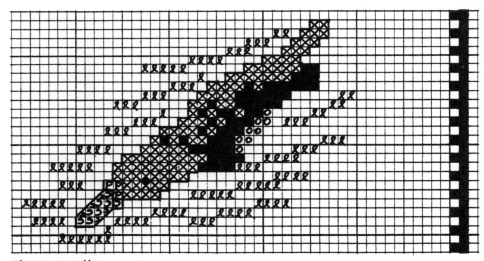

Platypus motif

ᘛ blue
▪ chocolate brown
✕ brown
P peach
つ grey/brown
O fawn

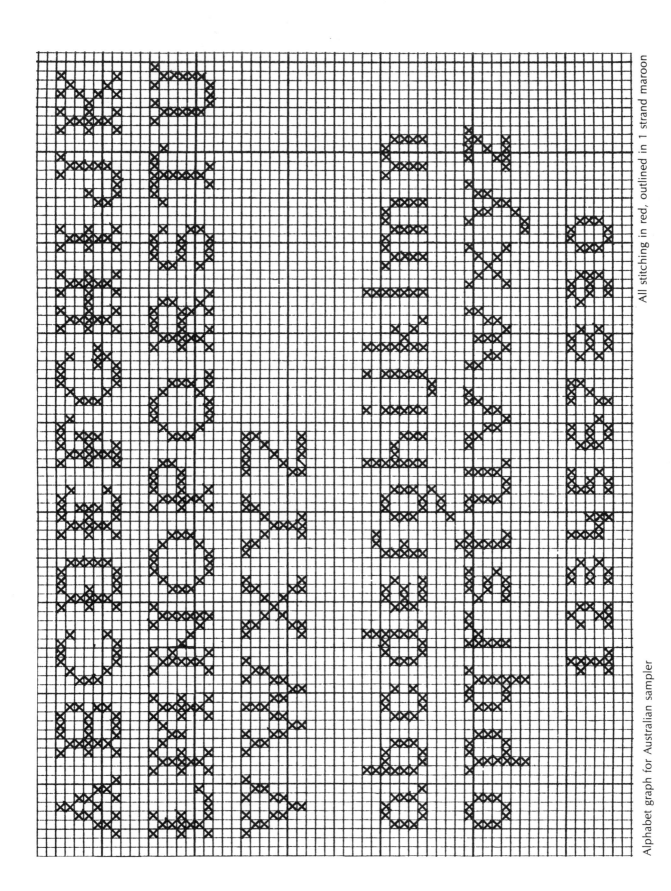

All stitching in red, outlined in 1 strand maroon

Alphabet graph for Australian sampler

Index